# The Poetry Of Charlotte Perkins Gilman

Charlotte Perkins Gilman (July 3, 1860 – August 17, 1935) was a prominent American sociologist, novelist, writer of short stories, poetry, and nonfiction, and a lecturer for social reform. She was a utopian feminist during a time when her accomplishments were exceptional for women, and she served as a role model for future generations of feminists because of her unorthodox concepts and lifestyle. Her best remembered work today is her semi-autobiographical short story, "The Yellow Wallpaper", which she wrote after a severe bout of postpartum psychosis.

## Index Of Poems

A Common Inference

A night: mysterious, tender, quiet, deep;
Heavy with flowers; full of life asleep;
Thrilling with insect voices; thick with stars;
No cloud between the dewdrops and red Mars;
The small earth whirling softly on her way,
The moonbeams and the waterfalls at play;
A million million worlds that move in peace,
A million mighty laws that never cease;
And one small ant-heap, hidden by small weeds,
Rich with eggs, slaves, and store of millet seeds.
They sleep beneath the sod
And trust in God.

A day: all glorious, royal, blazing bright;
Heavy with flowers; full of life and light;
Great fields of corn and sunshine; courteous trees;
Snow-sainted mountains; earth-embracing seas;
Wide golden deserts; slender silver streams;
Clear rainbows where the tossing fountain gleams;
And everywhere, in happiness and peace,
A million forms of life that never cease;
And one small ant-heap, crushed by passing tread,
Hath scarce enough alive to mourn the dead!
They shriek beneath the sod,
"There is no God!"


## A Conservative

The garden beds I wandered by
One bright and cheerful morn,
When I found a new-fledged butterfly,
A-sitting on a thorn,
A black and crimson butterfly
All doleful and forlorn.

I thought that life could have no sting
To infant butterflies,
So I gazed on this unhappy thing
With wonder and surprise.
While sadly with his waving wing
He wiped his weeping eyes.

Said I, 'What can the matter be?
Why weepest thou so sore?
With garden fair and sunlight free
And flowers in goodly store,'
But he only turned away from me
And burst into a roar.

Cried he, 'My legs are thin and few
Where once I had a swarm!

Soft fuzzy fur — a joy to view
Once kept my body warm,
Before these flapping wing-things grew,
To hamper and deform!'

At that outrageous bug I shot
The fury of mine eye;
Said I, in scorn all burning hot,
In rage and anger high,
'You ignominious idiot!
Those wings are made to fly!'

'I do not want to fly,' said he,
'I only want to squirm!'
And he drooped his wings dejectedly,
But still his voice was firm:
'I do not want to be a fly!
I want to be a worm!

O yesterday of unknown lack
To-day of unknown bliss!
I left my fool in red and black;
The last I saw was this,
The creature madly climbing back
Into his chrysalis.


## A Question

Why is it, God, that mother's hearts are made
So very deep and wide?
How does it help the world that we should hold
Such swelling floods of pain till we are old,
Because when we were young one grave was laid
One baby died?


## Another Star

There are five a-light before us,
In the flag flying o'er us,
There'll be six on next election
We bring a new star!
We are coming like the others,
Free Sisters, Free Brothers,
In the pride of our affection
For California.
CHORUS: A ballot for the Lady!
For the Home and for the Baby!
Come, vote ye for the Lady,
The Baby, the Home!

Star of Hope and Star of Beauty!
Of Freedom! Of Duty!
Star of childhood's new protection,
That rises so high!
We will work for it together
In the golden, gay weather,
And we'll have it next election,
Or we will know why.
CHORUS: A ballot for the Lady!
For the Home and for the Baby!
Come, vote ye for the Lady,
The Baby, the Home!

## Boys Will Be Boys

'Boys will be boys,' and boys have had their day;
Boy - mischief and boy - carelessness and noise
Extenuated all, allowed, excused and smoothed away,
Each duty missed, each damaging wild act,
By this meek statement of unquestioned fact
Boys will be boys!

Now, 'women will be women.' Mark the change;
Calm motherhood in place of boisterous youth;
No warfare now; to manage and arrange,
To nurture with wise care, is woman's way,
In peace and fruitful industry her sway,
In love and truth.

## Coming

Because the time is ripe, the age is ready,
Because the world her woman's help demands,
Out of the long subjection and seclusion
Come to our field of warfare and confusion
The mother's heart and hands.

Long has she stood aside, endured and waited,
While man swung forward, toiling on alone;
Now, for the weary man, so long ill-mated,
Now, for the world for which she was created,
Comes woman to her own.

Not for herself! though sweet the air of freedom;
Not for herself, though dear the new-born power;
But for the child, who needs a nobler mother,
For the whole people, needing one another,
Comes woman to her hour.

What an exceeding rest 'twill be
When I can leave off being Me!
To think of it! — at last be rid
Of all the things I ever did!

Done with the varying distress
Of retroactive consciousness!
Set free to feel the joy unknown
Of Life and Love beyond my own!

Why should I long to have John Smith
Eternally to struggle with?
I'm John — but somehow cherubim
Seem quite incongruous with him.

It would not seem so queer to dwell
Eternally John Smith in Hell.
To be one man forever seems
Most fit in purgatorial dreams.

But Heaven! Rest and Power and Peace
Must surely mean the soul's release
From this small labeled entity
This passing limitation — Me!


## Females

The female fox she is a fox;
The female whale a whale;
The female eagle holds her place
As representative of race
As truly as the male.

The mother hen doth scratch for her chicks,
And scratch for herself beside;
The mother cow doth nurse her calf,
Yet fares as well as her other half
In the pasture far and wide.

The female bird doth soar in air;
The female fish doth swim;
The fleet-foot mare upon the course
Doth hold her own with the flying horse
Yea and she beateth him!

One female in the world we find
Telling a different tale.
It is the female of our race,
Who holds a parasitic place

Dependent on the male.

Not so, saith she, ye slander me!
No parasite am I.
I earn my living as a wife;
My children take my very life;
Why should I share in human strife,
To plant and build and buy?

The human race holds highest place
In all the world so wide,
Yet these inferior females wive,
And raise their little ones alive,
And feed themselves beside.

Thre race is higher than the sex,
Though sex be fair and good;
A Human Creature is your state,
And to be human is more great
Than even womanhood!

The female fox she is a fox;
The female whale a whale;
The female eagle holds her place
As representative of race
As truly as the male.


For Fear
For fear of prowling beasts at night
They blocked the cave;
Women and children hid from sight,
Men scarce more brave.

For fear of warrior's sword and spear
They barred the gate;
Women and children lived in fear,
Men lived in hate.

For fear of criminals today
We lock the door;
Women and children still to stay
Hid evermore.

Come out! Ye need no longer hide!
What fear you now?
No wolf or lion waits outside
Only a cow.

Come out! The world approaches peace,
War nears its end;

No warrior watches your release
Only a friend.

Come out! The night of crime has fled
Day is begun;
Here is no criminal to dread
Only your son.

The world, half yours, demands your care,
Waken and come!
Make it a woman's world; safe, fair,
Garden and home.


### Girls Of To-Day

Girls of today! Give ear!
Never since time began
Has come to the race of man
A year, a day, an hour,
So full of promise and power
As the time that now is here!

Never in all the lands
Was there a power so great,
To move the wheels of state,
To lift up body and mind,
To waken the deaf and blind,
As the power that is in your hands!

Here at the gates of gold
You stand in the pride of youth,
Strong in courage and truth,
Stirred by a force kept back
Through centuries long and black,
Armed with a power threefold!

First: You are makers of men!
Then Be the things you preach!
Let your own greatness teach!
When Mothers like this you see
Men will be strong and free
Then, and not till then!

Second: Since Adam fell,
Have you not heard it said
That men by women are led?
True is the saying–true!
See to it what you do!
See that you lead them well.

Third: You have work of your own!

Maid and mother and wife,
Look in the face of life!
There are duties you owe the race!
Outside your dwelling-place
There is work for you alone!

Maid and mother and wife,
See your own work be done!
Be worthy a noble son!
Help man in the upward way!
Truly, a girl today
Is the strongest thing in life!


## Locked Inside

She beats upon her bolted door,
With faint weak hands;
Drearily walks the narrow floor;
Sullenly sits, blank walls before;
Despairing stands.

Life calls her, Duty, Pleasure, Gain
Her dreams respond;
But the blank daylights wax and wane,
Dull peace, sharp agony, slow pain
No hope beyond.

Till she comes a thought! She lifts her head,
The world grows wide!
A voice – as if clear words were said
'Your door, O long imprisonéd,
Is locked inside!'


## Mother To Child

How best can I serve thee, my child! My child!
Flesh of my flesh and dear heart of my heart!
Once thou wast within me – I held thee – I fed thee
By the force of my loving and longing I led thee
Now we are apart!

I may blind thee with kisses and crush with embracing,
Thy warm mouth in my neck and our arms interlacing;
But here in my body my soul lives alone,
And thou answerest me from a house of thine own
The house which I builded!

Which we builded together, thy father and I;
In which thou must live, O my darling, and die!
Not one stone can I alter, one atom relay

Not to save or defend thee or help thee to stay
That gift is completed!

How best can I serve thee? O child, if they knew
How my heart aches with loving! How deep and how true,
How brave and enduring, how patient, how strong,
How longing for good and how fearful of wrong,
Is the love of thy mother!

Could I crown thee with riches! Surround, overflow thee
With fame and with power till the whole world should know thee;
With wisdom and genius to hold the world still,
To bring laughter and tears, joy and pain, at thy will,
Still – thou mightst not be happy!

Such have lived–and in sorrow. The greater the mind
The wider and deeper the grief it can find.
The richer, the gladder, the more thou canst feel
The keen stings that a lifetime is sure to reveal.
O my child! Must thou suffer?

Is there no way my life can save thine from a pain?
Is the love of a mother no possible gain?
No labor of Hercules – search for the Grail
No way for this wonderful love to avail?
God in Heaven – O teach me!

My prayer has been answered. The pain thou must bear
Is the pain of the world's life which thy life must share,
Thou art one with the world – though I love thee the best;
And to save thee from pain I must save all the rest–
Well – with God's help I'll do it.

Thou art one with the rest. I must love thee in them.
Thou wilt sin with the rest; and thy mother must stem
The world's sin. Thou wilt weep, and thy mother must dry
The tears of the world lest her darling should cry.
I will do it – God helping!

And I stand not alone. I will gather a band
Of all loving mothers from land unto land.
Our children are part of the world! Do ye hear?
They are one with the world – we must hold them all dear!
Love all for the child's sake!

For the sake of my child I must hasten to save
All the children on earth from the jail and the grave.
For so, and so only, I lighten the share
Of the pain of the world that my darling must bear
Even so, and so only!

## Nation

The nation is the unit. That which makes
You an American of our Today,
Requires this nation and its history,
Requires the sum of all our citizens,
Requires the product of our common toil,
Requires the freedom of our common laws,
The common heart of our humanity.

Decrease our population, check our growth,
Deprive us of our wealth, our liberty,
Lower the nation's conscience by a hair,
And you are less than that you were before!
You stand here in the world the man you are,
Because your country is America!

Our liberty belongs to each of us:
The nation guarantees it; in return
We serve the nation, serving so ourselves.
Our education is a common right;
The state provides it, equally to all,
Each taking what he can; and in return
We serve the state, so serving best ourselves.
Food, clothing, all necessities of life
These are a right as much as liberty!
The nation feeds its children. In return
We serve the nation, serving still ourselves.
Nay, not ourselves — ourself! We are but parts.
The unit is the state — America!

## Now

With God Above – Beneath – Beside
Without – Within – and Everywhere;
Rising with the resistless tide
Of life, and Sure of Getting There.

Patient with Nature's long delay,
Proud of our conscious upward swing;
Not sorry for a single day,
And Not Afraid of Anything!

With Motherhood at last awake
With Power to Do and Light to See
Women may now begin to Make
The People we are Meant to Be!

## Reassurance

Can you imagine nothing better, brother,
Than that which you have always had before?
Have you been so content with 'wife and mother,'
You dare hope nothing more?

Have you forever prized her, praised her, sung her,
The happy queen of a most happy reign?
Never dishonored her, despised her, flung her
Derision and disdain?

Go ask the literature of all the ages!
Books that were written before women read!
Pagan and Christian, satirists and sages
Read what the world has said.

There was no power on earth to bid you slacken
The generous hand that painted her disgrace!
There was no shame on earth too black to blacken
That much-praised woman-face.

Eve and Pandora!–always you begin it
The ancients called her Sin and Shame and Death.
'There is no evil without woman in it,'
The modern proverb saith.

She has been yours in uttermost possession
Your slave, your mother, your well-chosen bride
And you have owned in million-fold confession,
You were not satisfied.

Peace then! Fear not the coming woman, brother.
Owning herself, she giveth all the more.
She shall be better woman, wife and mother,
Than man hath known before.


## She Walketh Veiled And Sleeping

She walketh veiled and sleeping,
For she knoweth not her power;
She obeyeth but the pleading
Of her heart, and the high leading
Of her soul, unto this hour.
Slow advancing, halting, creeping,
Comes the Woman to the hour!
She walketh veiled and sleeping,
For she knoweth not her power.


## She Who Is To Come

A woman—in so far as she beholdeth
Her one Beloved's face;
A mother—with a great heart that enfoldeth
The children of the Race;
A body, free and strong, with that high beauty
That comes of perfect use, is built thereof;
A mind where Reason ruleth over Duty,
And Justice reigns with Love;
A self-poised, royal soul, brave, wise and tender,
No longer blind and dumb;
A Human Being, of an unknown splendor,
Is she who is to come!


## Similar Cases

There was once a little animal,
No bigger than a fox,
And on five toes he scampered
Over Tertiary rocks.
They called him Eohippus,
And they called him very small,
And they thought him of no value
When they thought of him at all;
For the lumpish old Dinoceras
And Coryphodon so slow
Were the heavy aristocracy
In days of long ago.

Said the little Eohippus,
'I am going to be a horse!
And on my middle finger-nails
To run my earthly course!
I'm going to have a flowing tail!
I'm going to have a mane!
I'm going to stand fourteen hands high
On the psychozoic plain!'

The Coryphodon was horrified,
The Dinoceras was shocked;
And they chased young Eohippus,
But he skipped away and mocked.
And they laughed enormous laughter,
And they groaned enormous groans,
And they bade young Eohippus
Go view his father's bones.
Said they, 'You always were as small
And mean as now we see,
And that's conclusive evidence
That you're always going to be.
What! Be a great, tall, handsome beast,
With hoofs to gallop on?

Why! You'd have to change your nature!'
Said the Loxolophodon.
They considered him disposed of,
And retired with gait serene;
That was the way they argued
In 'the early Eocene.'
There was once an Anthropoidal Ape,
Far smarter than the rest,
And everything that they could do
He always did the best;
So they naturally disliked him,
And they gave him shoulders cool,
And when they had to mention him
They said he was a fool.
Cried this pretentious Ape one day,
'I'm going to be a Man!
And stand upright, and hunt, and fight,
And conquer all I can!
I'm going to cut down forest trees,
To make my houses higher!
I'm going to kill the Mastodon!
I'm going to make a fire!'
Loud screamed the Anthropoidal Apes
With laughter wild and gay;
They tried to catch that boastful one,
But he always got away.
So they yelled at him in chorus,
Which he minded not a whit;
And they pelted him with cocoanuts,
Which didn't seem to hit.
And then they gave him reasons
Which they thought of much avail,
To prove how his preposterous
Attempt was sure to fail.
Said the sages, 'In the first place,
The thing cannot be done!
And, second, if it could be,
It would not be any fun!
And, third, and most conclusive,
And admitting no reply,
You would have to change your nature!
We should like to see you try!'
They chuckled then triumphantly,
These lean and hairy shapes,
For these things passed as arguments
With the Anthropoidal Apes.
There was once a Neolithic Man,
An enterprising wight,
Who made his chopping implements
Unusually bright.
Unusually clever he,
Unusually brave,

And he drew delightful Mammoths
On the borders of his cave.
To his Neolithic neighbors,
Who were startled and surprised,
Said he, 'My friends, in course of time,
We shall be civilized!
We are going to live in cities!
We are going to fight in wars!
We are going to eat three times a day
Without the natural cause!
We are going to turn life upside down
About a thing called gold!
We are going to want the earth, and take
As much as we can hold!
We are going to wear great piles of stuff
Outside our proper skins!
We are going to have diseases!
And Accomplishments!! And Sins!!!'

Then they all rose up in fury
Against their boastful friend,
For prehistoric patience
Cometh quickly to an end.
Said one, 'This is chimerical!
Utopian! Absurd!'
Said another, 'What a stupid life!
Too dull, upon my word!'
Cried all, 'Before such things can come,
You idiotic child,
You must alter Human Nature!'
And they all sat back and smiled.
Thought they, 'An answer to that last
It will be hard to find!'
It was a clinching argument
To the Neolithic Mind!


## Song For Equal Suffrage

Day of hope and day of glory! After slavery and woe,
Comes the dawn of woman's freedom, and the light shall grow and grow
Until every man and woman equal liberty shall know,
In Freedom marching on!

Woman's right is woman's duty! For our share in life we call!
Our will it is not weakened and our power it is not small.
We are half of every nation! We are mothers of them all!
In Wisdom marching on!

Not for self but larger service has our cry for freedom grown,
There is crime, disease and warfare in a world of men alone,
In the name of love we're rising now to serve and save our own,

As Peace comes marching on!

By every sweet and tender tie around our heartstrings curled,
In the cause of nobler motherhood is woman's flag unfurled,
Till every child shall know the joy and peace of mother's world–
As Love comes marching on!

We will help to make a pruning hook of every outgrown sword,
We will help to knit the nations in continuing accord,
In humanity made perfect is the glory of the Lord,
As His world goes marching on!


## The

The fly upon the Cartwheel
Thought she made all the Sound;
He thought he made the Cart go on
And made the wheels go round.

The Fly upon the Cartwheel
Has won undying fame
For Conceit that was colossal,
And Ignorance the same.

But today he has a Rival
As we roll down History's Track
For the 'Anti' on the Cartwheel
Thinks she makes the Wheels go back!


## The Anti-Suffragists

Fashionable women in luxurious homes,
With men to feed them, clothe them, pay their bills,
Bow, doff the hat, and fetch the handkerchief;
Hostess or guest; and always so supplied
With graceful deference and courtesy;
Surrounded by their horses, servants, dogs
These tell us they have all the rights they want.

Successful women who have won their way
Alone, with strength of their unaided arm,
Or helped by friends, or softly climbing up
By the sweet aid of 'woman's influence';
Successful any way, and caring naught
For any other woman's unsuccess
These tell us they have all the rights they want.

Religious women of the feebler sort
Not the religion of a righteous world,
A free, enlightened, upward-reaching world,

But the religion that considers life
As something to back out of! whose ideal
Is to renounce, submit, and sacrifice.
Counting on being patted on the head
And given a high chair when they get to heaven
These tell us they have all the rights they want.

Ignorant women – college bred sometimes,
But ignorant of life's realities
And principles of righteous government,
And how the privileges they enjoy
Were won with blood and tears by those before
Those they condemn, whose ways they now oppose;
Saying, 'Why not let well enough alone?'
Our world is very pleasant as it is'
These tell us they have all the rights they want.

And selfish women – pigs in petticoats
Rich, poor, wise, unwise, top or bottom round,
But all sublimely innocent of thought,
And guiltless of ambition, save the one
Deep, voiceless aspiration – to be fed!
These have no use for rights or duties more.
Duties today are more than they can meet,
And law insures their right to clothes and food
These tell us they have all the rights they want.

And, more's the pity, some good women too;
Good, conscientious women with ideas;
Who think–or think they think–that woman's cause
Is best advanced by letting it alone;
That she somehow is not a human thing,

And not to be helped on by human means,
Just added to humanity – an 'L'
A wing, a branch, an extra, not mankind
These tell us they have all the rights they want.

And out of these has come a monstrous thing,
A strange, down-sucking whirlpool of disgrace,
Women uniting against womanhood,
And using that great name to hide their sin!
Vain are their words as that old king's command
Who set his will against the rising tide.
But who shall measure the historic shame
Of these poor traitors–traitors are they all
To great Democracy and Womanhood!

The Beds of Fleur-de-Lys

High lying, sea-blown stretches of green turf,
Wind-bitten close, salt-colored by the sea,
Low curve on curve spread far to the cool sky,
And, curving over them as long they lie,
Beds of wild fleur-de-lys.

Wide-flowing, self-sown, stealing near and far,
Breaking the green like islands in the sea;
Great stretches at your feet, and spots that bend
Dwindling over the horizon's end,
Wild beds of fleur-de-lys.

The light keen wind streams on across the lifts,
Their wind of western springtime by the sea;
The close turf smiles unmoved, but over her
Is the far-flying rustle and sweet stir
In beds of fleur-de-lys.

And here and there across the smooth, low grass
Tall maidens wander, thinking of the sea;
And bend, and bend, with light robes blown aside,
For the blue lily-flowers that bloom so wide,
The beds of fleur-de-lys.


## The Housewife

Here is the House to hold me – cradle of all the race;
Here is my lord and my love, here are my children dear
Here is the House enclosing, the dear-loved dwelling place;
Why should I ever weary for aught that I find not here?

Here for the hours of the day and the hours of the night;
Bound with the bands of Duty, rivetted tight;
Duty older than Adam – Duty that saw
Acceptance utter and hopeless in the eyes of the serving squaw.

Food and the serving of food – that is my daylong care;
What and when we shall eat, what and how we shall wear;
Soiling and cleaning of things – that is my task in the main
Soil them and clean them and soil them – soil them and clean them again.

To work at my trade by the dozen and never a trade to know;
To plan like a Chinese puzzle–fitting and changing so;
To think of a thousand details, each in a thousand ways;
For my own immediate people and a possible love and praise.

My mind is trodden in circles, tiresome, narrow and hard,
Useful, commonplace, private – simply a small backyard;
And I the Mother of Nations! Blind their struggle and vain!
I cover the earth with my children – each with a housewife's brain.

## The Malingerer

Exempt! She 'does not have to work!'
So might one talk
Defending long, bedridden ease,
Weak yielding ankles, flaccid knees,
With 'I don't have to walk!'

Not have to work. Why not? Who gave
Free pass to you?
You're housed and fed and taught and dressed
By age-long labor of the rest
Work other people do!

What do you give in honest pay
For clothes and food?
Then as a shield, defence, excuse,
She offers her exclusive use
Her function – Motherhood!

Is motherhood a trade you make
A living by?
And does the wealth you so may use,
Squander, accumulate, abuse,
Show motherhood as high?

Or does the motherhood of those
Whose toil endures,
The farmers' and mechanics' wives,
Hard working servants all their lives
Deserve less price than yours?

We're not exempt! Man's world runs on,
Motherless, wild;
Our servitude and long duress,
Our shameless, harem idleness,
Both fail to serve the child.

## The Socialist And The Suffragist

Said the Socialist to the Suffragist:
'My cause is greater than yours!
You only work for a Special Class,
We work for the gain of the General Mass,
Which every good ensures!'

Said the Suffragist to the Socialist:
'You underrate my Cause!
While women remain a Subject Class,
You never can move the General Mass,

With your Economic Laws!'

Said the Socialist to the Suffragist:
'You misinterpret facts!
There is no room for doubt or schism
In Economic Determinism
It governs all our acts!'

Said the Suffragist to the Socialist:
'You men will always find
That this old world will never move
More swiftly in its ancient groove
While women stay behind! '

'A lifted world lifts women up,'
The Socialist explained.
'You cannot lift the world at all
While half of it is kept so small,'
The Suffragist maintained.

The world awoke, and tartly spoke:
'Your work is all the same:
Work together or work apart,
Work, each of you, with all your heart
Just get into the game!'


### The Wolf At The Door

There's a haunting horror near us
That nothing drives away;
Fierce lamping eyes at nightfall,
A crouching shade by day;
There's a whining at the threshold,
There's a scratching at the floor.
To work! To work! In Heaven's name!
The wolf is at the door!

The day was long, the night was short,
The bed was hard and cold;
Still weary are the little ones,
Still weary are the old.

We are weary in our cradles
From our mother's toil untold;
We are born to hoarded weariness
As some to hoarded gold.

We will not rise! We will not work!
Nothing the day can give
Is half so sweet an hour of sleep;
Better to sleep than live!

What power can stir these heavy limbs?
What hope these dull hearts swell?
What fear more cold, what pain more sharp
Than the life we know so well?

The slow, relentless, padding step
That never goes astray
The rustle in the underbrush
The shadow in the way
The straining flight, the long pursuit
The steady gain behind
Death-wearied man and tireless brute,
And the struggle wild and blind!

There's a hot breath at the keyhole
And a tearing as of teeth!
Well do I know the bloodshot eyes
And the dripping jaws beneath!
There's a whining at the threshold
There's a scratching at the floor
To work! To work! In Heaven's name!
The wolf is at the door!


## To The Indifferent Women

You who are happy in a thousand homes,
Or overworked therein, to a dumb peace;
Whose souls are wholly centered in the life
Of that small group you personally love
Who told you that you need not know or care
About the sin and sorrow of the world?

Do you believe the sorrow of the world
Does not concern you in your little homes?
That you are licensed to avoid the care
And toil for human progress, human peace,
And the enlargement of our power of love
Until it covers every field of life?

The one first duty of all human life
Is to promote the progress of the world
In righteousness, in wisdom, truth and love;
And you ignore it, hidden in your homes,
Content to keep them in uncertain peace,
Content to leave all else without your care.

Yet you are mothers! And a mother's care
Is the first step towards friendly human life.
Life where all nations in untroubled peace
Unite to raise the standard of the world
And make the happiness we seek in homes

Spread everywhere in strong and fruitful love.

You are content to keep that mighty love
In its first steps forever; the crude care
Of animals for mate and young and homes,
Instead of poring it abroad in life,
Its mighty current feeding all the world
Till every human child shall grow in peace.

You cannot keep your small domestic peace,
Your little pool of undeveloped love,
While the neglected, starved, unmothered world
Struggles and fights for lack of mother's care,
And its tempestuous, bitter, broken life
Beats in upon you in your selfish homes.

We all may have our homes in joy and peace
When woman's life, in its rich power of love
Is joined with man's to care for all the world!


**Up And Down**
Up, up up! On and out and away
From the little beast I live in,
Through the sweet home life I give in,
With its dear, close love;
Out of that fragrant gloom,
With its crowding fruit and bloom,
Into the wide clear day;
Into the world above.

Out, where the soul can spread
Into the lives of many
Feeling the joy and pain,
The peace, the toil, the strain
That is not spared to any;
Feeling and working as one;
So is our life begun
The life that can never grow
Till it has widened so.
The neighborless soul is dead.

On — with a sharp-caught breath,
Into the space beyond
Wonderful white-blue space
Where you feel through shifting time
The slow-formed life sublime
Of a yet unconscious race.
Where you live beyond all tears;
Where centuries slide as years
And the flickering screen of death

Shows God's face calm and fond.

Even — a moment's dream
A flash that lifts and flies
Even beyond our brothers
To a day when the full-born soul,
World circling, conscious, whole,
Shall taste the world's full worth
Shall feel the swing of the earth
Feel what life will seem
When we walk the thronging skies
And the earth shall sing with the others!

Down, down, down! Back and in and home!
Circling softly through
The spaces vast and blue;
The centuries' whirling spokes
Settling back again
To time-marks clear and plain,
As we count the separate strokes.
The race lifelong and free
Narrowed to what we see,
Our own set hope and power
In the history of the hour
Back to our time we come.

In, where the Soul is warm
With the clinging, lingering touch
Of those we love so much,
And the daring wings can rest;
Back, where the task is small,
Easy and plain to all,
The life that most hold best
Humanity's first form.

Down! If we fail of this;
Down to the very base
The Universe, the Race,
Country and Friends and Home
Here at the end we come
To the first gift that was given,
The little beast we live in!
Rest and be happy, soul!
This was an age-long goal,
This too you may nobly love
Failing of aught above;
Feeling that, even here,
Life is as true, as near,
As one with the will of God
As sky, or sea, or sod
Or aught of the world that is.

## We As Women

There's a cry in the air about us
We hear it, before, behind
Of the way in which 'We, as women,'
Are going to lift mankind!

With our white frocks starched and ruffled,
And our soft hair brushed and curled
Hats off! for 'We, as women,'
Are coming to save the world.

Fair sisters! listen one moment
And perhaps you'll pause for ten:
The business of women as women
Is only with men as men!

What we do, 'We, as women,'
We have done all through our life;
The work that is ours as women
Is the work of mother and wife.

But to elevate public opinion,
And to lift up erring man,
Is the work of the Human Being;
Let us do it – if we can.

But wait, warm-hearted sisters
Not quite so fast, so far.
Tell me how we are going to lift a thing
Any higher than we are!

We are going to 'purify politics,'
And to 'elevate the press.'
We enter the foul paths of the world
To sweeten and cleanse and bless.

To hear the high things we are going to do,
And the horrors of man we tell,
One would think, 'We, as women,' were angels,
And our brothers were fiends of hell.

We, that were born of one mother,
And reared in the self-same place,
In the school and the church together,
We of one blood, one race!

Now then, all forward together!
But remember, every one,
That 'tis not by feminine innocence
The work of the world is done.

The world needs strength and courage,
And wisdom to help and feed
When, 'We, as women' bring these to man,
We shall lift the world indeed.


## Wedded Bliss

'O come and be my mate!' said the Eagle to the Hen,
'I love to soar, but then
I want my mate to rest
Forever in the nest!'
Said the Hen, 'I cannot fly,
I have no wish to try,
But I joy to see my mate careening through the sky!'
They wed, and cried, 'Ah, this is Love, my own!'
And the Hen sat, the Eagle soared, alone.

'O come and be my mate!' said the Lion to the Sheep;
'My love for you is deep!
I slay, a Lion should,
But you are mild and good!'
Said the sheep, 'I do no ill
Could not, had I the will.
But I joy to see my mate pursue, devour and kill.'
They wed, and cried, 'Ah, this is Love, my own!'
And the Sheep browsed, the Lion prowled, alone.

'O come and be my mate!' said the Salmon to the Clam;
'You are not wise, but I am.
I know sea and stream as well.
You know nothing but your shell.'
Said the Clam, 'I'm slow of motion,
But my love is all devotion,
And I joy to have my mate traverse lake and stream and ocean!'
They wed, and cried, 'Ah, this is Love, my own!'
And the Clam sucked, the Salmon swam, alone.


## Women Do Not Want It

When the woman suffrage argument first stood upon its legs,
They answered it with cabbages, they answered it with eggs,
They answered it with ridicule, they answered it with scorn,
They thought it a monstrosity that should not have been born.

When the woman suffrage argument grew vigorous and wise,
And was not to be answered by these opposite replies,
They turned their opposition into reasoning severe
Upon the limitations of our God-appointed sphere.

We were told of disabilities – a long array of these,
Till one could think that womanhood was merely a disease;
And 'the maternal sacrifice' was added to the plan
Of the various sacrifices we have always made–to man.

Religionists and scientists, in amity and bliss,
However else they disagreed, could all agree on this,
And the gist of all their discourse, when you got down in it,
Was–we could not have the ballot because we were not fit!

They would not hear the reason, they would not fairly yield,
They would not own their arguments were beaten in the field;
But time passed on, and someway, we need not ask them how,
Whatever ails those arguments–we do not hear them now!

You may talk of suffrage now with an educated man,
And he agrees with all you say, as sweetly as he can:
'T would be better for us all, of course, if womanhood was free;
But 'the women do not want it' – and so it must not be!

'T is such a tender thoughtfulness! So exquisite a care!
Not to pile on our frail shoulders what we do not wish to bear!
But, oh, most generous brother! Let us look a little more
Have we women always wanted what you gave to us before?

Did we ask for veils and harems in the Oriental races?
Did we beseech to be 'unclean,' shut out of sacred places?
Did we beg for scolding bridles and ducking stools to come?
And clamour for the beating stick no thicker than your thumb?

Did we ask to be forbidden from all the trades that pay?
Did we claim the lower wages for a man's full work today?
Have we petitioned for the laws wherein our shame is shown:
That not a woman's child – nor her own body – is her own?

What women want has never been a strongly acting cause,
When woman has been wronged by man in churches, customs, laws;
Why should he find this preference so largely in his way,
When he himself admits the right of what we ask today?


Women Of To-Day

You women of today who fear so much
The women of the future, showing how
The dangers of her course are such and such
What are you now?

Mothers and Wives and Housekeepers, forsooth!
Great names, you cry, full scope to rule and please,
Room for wise age and energetic youth!
But are you these?

Housekeepers? Do you then, like those of yore,
Keep house with power and pride, with grace and ease?
No, you keep servants only! What is more
You don't keep these!

Wives, say you? Wives! Blessed indeed are they
Who hold of love the everlasting keys,
Keeping your husbands' hearts! Alas the day!
You don't keep these!

And mothers? Pitying Heaven! Mark the cry
From cradle death-beds! Mothers on their knees!
Why, half the children born, as children, die!
You don't keep these!

And still the wailing babies come and go,
And homes are waste, and husband's hearts fly far;
There is no hope until you dare to know
The thing you are!


### Women To Men

Dear father, from my cradle I acknowledge
All your wise kindness, tender care, and love,
Through days of kindergarten, school, and college.
Now there is one gift lacking – one above
All other gifts of God, this highest trust is,
The one great gift, beyond all power and pelf
Give me my freedom, father; give me justice,
That I may guard my children and myself.

My brother, you and I were reared together;
We played together, even-handed quite;
We went to school in every kind of weather,
Studied and ranked together as was right.
We work together now and earn our living,
You know how equal is the work we do;
Come, brother, with the love you're always giving,
Give justice! It's for me as well as you.

And you, my lover, kneeling here before me
With tender eyes that burn, warm lips that plead,
Protesting that you worship, aye, adore me;
Begging my love as life's supremest meed,
Vowing to make me happy. Ah, how dare you!
Freedom and happiness have both one key!
Lover and husband, by the love I bear you,
Give justice! I can love you better, free!

Son, my own son! Man-child that once was lying

All rosy, tender, helpless on my breast,
Your strength, all dimples, your stern voice but crying,
Looking to me for comfort, food and rest,
Asking your life of me, and not another
And asking not in vain till life be done
Oh, my boy-baby! Is it I, your mother,
Who comes to ask of justice from her son?

Now to the voter – tax-payer (or shirker)
Please lay your private feelings on the shelf;
O Man-at-large! Friend! Comrade! Fellow-worker;
I am a human being like yourself.
I'm not your wife and mother. Can't be, whether
I would or not: each to his own apart;
But in the world we're people altogether
Suffrage is not a question of the heart.

Son – Father – Brother – Lover unsupplanted
We'll talk at home. This thing concerns the nation;
A point of justice which is to be granted
By men to women who are no relation.
Perceive this fact, as salient as a steeple,
Please try to argue from it if you can;
Women have standing-room on earth as people
Outside of their relation to some man.

As wife and sweetheart, daughter, sister, mother,
Each woman privately her views explains;
As people of America, no other
We claim the right our government maintains.
You who deny it stand in history's pages
Withholding justice! Pitiless and plain
Your record stands down all the brightening ages
You fought with progress, but you fought in vain.

www.ingramcontent.com/pod-product-compliance
Lightning Source LLC
Chambersburg PA
CBHW070113070426
42448CB00038B/2659